Hidden Worlds

UNDER THE LIGHTS: EXPLORING THE SECRETS OF A Sports Stadium

by Tammy Enz

Reading Consultant:
Barbara J. Fox
Reading Specialist
North Carolina State University

Content Consultant:
Steven C. Maki, PE
Director of Facilities and Engineering
Metropolitan Sports Facilities Commission
Minneapolis, Minnesota

CAPSTONE PRESS
a capstone imprint

Blazers is published by Capstone Press,
151 Good Counsel Drive, P.O. Box 669, Mankato, Minnesota 56002.
www.capstonepress.com

Printed in the United States of America in Stevens Point, Wisconsin.
092009
005619WZS10

Books published by Capstone Press are manufactured with paper
containing at least 10 percent post-consumer waste.

Library of Congress Cataloging-in-Publication Data
Enz, Tammy.
      Under the lights : exploring the secrets of a sports stadium/by Tammy Enz.
      p. cm. — (Blazers: Hidden worlds)
      Summary: "Explores the behind-the-scenes places of a sports stadium" — Provided
by publisher.
      Includes bibliographical references and index.
      ISBN 978-1-4296-3376-5 (library binding)
      1. Stadiums — Juvenile literature. 2. Stadiums — Design and construction — Juvenile
literature. I. Title. II. Series.
GV415.E83 2010
725'.8043 — dc22   2008054992

Editorial Credits
Jennifer Besel, editor; Bobbie Nuytten and Veronica Bianchini, designers;
   Eric Gohl, media researcher; Laura Manthe, production specialist

Photo Credits
AP Images/Carolyn Kaster, cover; AP Images/Frank Franklin II, 15; AP Images/The Gazette, David
Wallace, 16 (inset); AP Images/Mel Evans, 9; AP Images/Mike Derer, 25; AP Images/Orlin Wagner,
21 (inset); AP Images/Reed Saxon, 24; AP Images/Tom Strickland, 27; Capstone Studio/Karon
Dubke, arena background and camera throughout, 7, 13, 16, 18, 21, 28; Getty Images Inc./AFP/
Stephane De Sakutin, 11; Getty Images Inc./AFP/Teh Eng Koon, 12; Getty Images Inc./Bongarts/
Christof Koepsel, 19; Getty Images Inc./Jed Jacobsohn, 6; Getty Images Inc./Ned Dishman, 22; Getty
Images Inc./Sports Illustrated/Greg Nelson, 14; Shutterstock/Andreas Bjerkeholt, throughout (concrete
texture); Shutterstock/ExaMedia Photography, 4; Shutterstock/Lagui, throughout (paper with tape);
Shutterstock/Pefkos, 10; Shutterstock/Pierre E. Debbas, 29; Shutterstock/Pokaz, throughout (grunge
background); Shutterstock/Robyn Mackenzie, throughout (paper); Shutterstock/WizData, Inc., 5

TABLE OF CONTENTS

CHAPTER 1

BEHIND THE STANDS

In the stands, the crowd goes wild for the home team. But there is even more activity off the field.

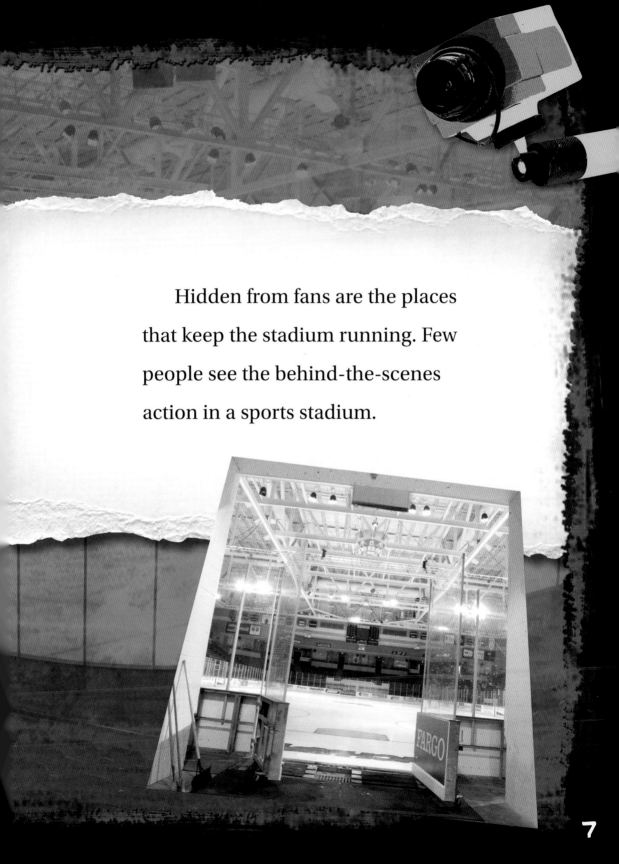

Hidden from fans are the places that keep the stadium running. Few people see the behind-the-scenes action in a sports stadium.

CHAPTER 2

AUTHORIZED PERSONNEL ONLY

Broadcast Center

Above the field, the **broadcast center** brings the game to people at home. Workers send the video out to TV stations. Workers also update the scoreboards on the field.

broadcast center — the place in the stadium that sends out a program to TV or radio stations

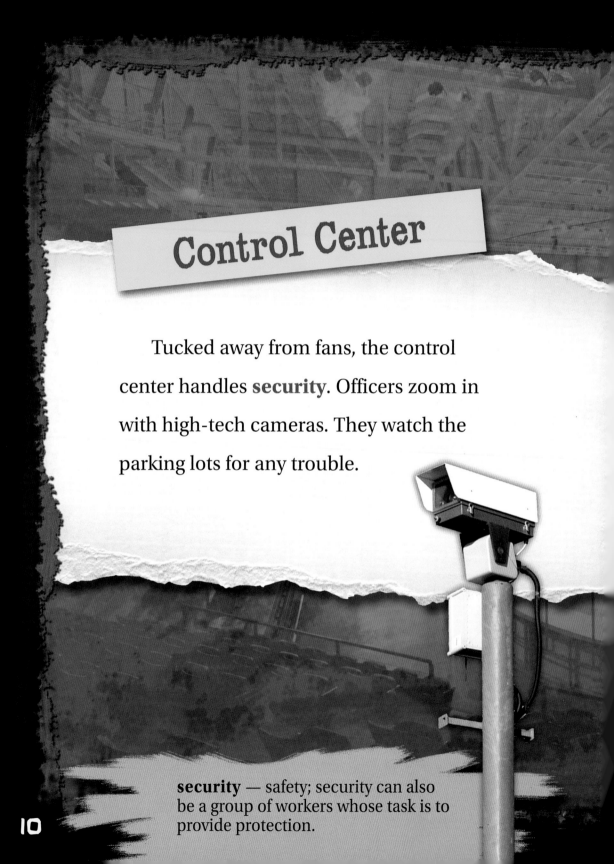

Control Center

Tucked away from fans, the control center handles **security**. Officers zoom in with high-tech cameras. They watch the parking lots for any trouble.

security — safety; security can also be a group of workers whose task is to provide protection.

INSIDE INFO

A stadium's security cameras can zoom in on people who are blocks away. Officers can even see through the windows of a car with these cameras.

WARNING!
Security Cameras Are Recording Activity In This Facility To Aid In The Prosecution Of Crime

Security staff can see anywhere in the stands from the control center. They type a section number into their computers. The camera zooms in. Officers see what's happening on **monitors**.

monitor — a TV or computer screen that is used to show what is being recorded

Home Team Locker Room

Away from screaming fans, home team players relax in the locker room. Leather couches and big-screen TVs line the walls. Players soak in the hot tubs.

INSIDE INFO

Some home team locker rooms even have
basketball courts and swimming pools.

Visiting Team's Locker Room

Down a long hallway, the visiting team gets a boring locker room. The only things in this room are lockers and showers.

INSIDE INFO

One college stadium has an all pink locker room for visitors. It has pink walls, carpet, and shower curtains.

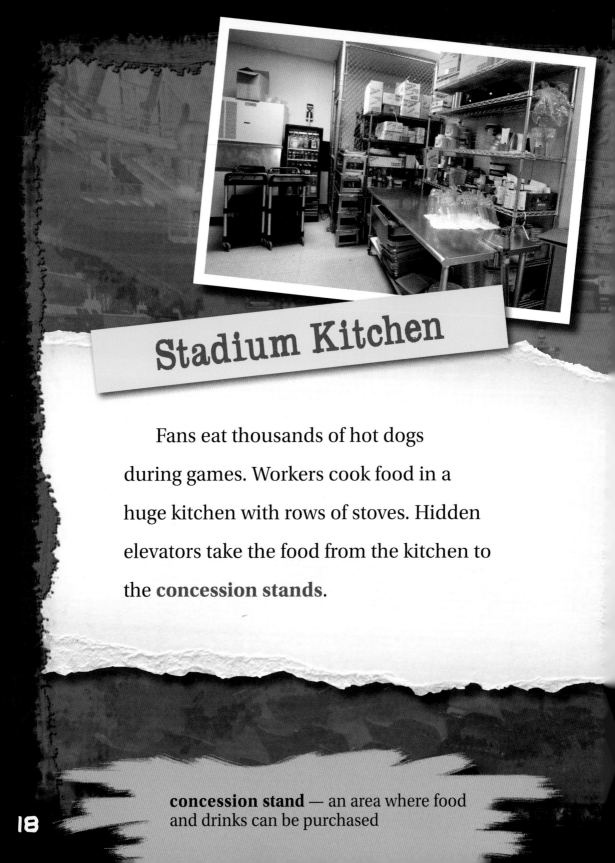

Stadium Kitchen

Fans eat thousands of hot dogs during games. Workers cook food in a huge kitchen with rows of stoves. Hidden elevators take the food from the kitchen to the **concession stands**.

concession stand — an area where food and drinks can be purchased

INSIDE INFO

Sports fans are hungry! At a major
college game, a kitchen will go through
25,000 hot dogs, 90 tons (82 metric tons)
of ice, and 3,000 cans of nacho cheese.

Maintenance Rooms

Hidden tunnels under the stadium lead to the **maintenance** rooms. Workers store equipment and supplies there. The maintenance rooms also have woodworking and welding shops to do stadium repairs.

maintenance — the upkeep of machines or a building

It takes a lot of paint to put the lines on a field. Workers use up to 100 gallons (379 liters) of paint for a single football game.

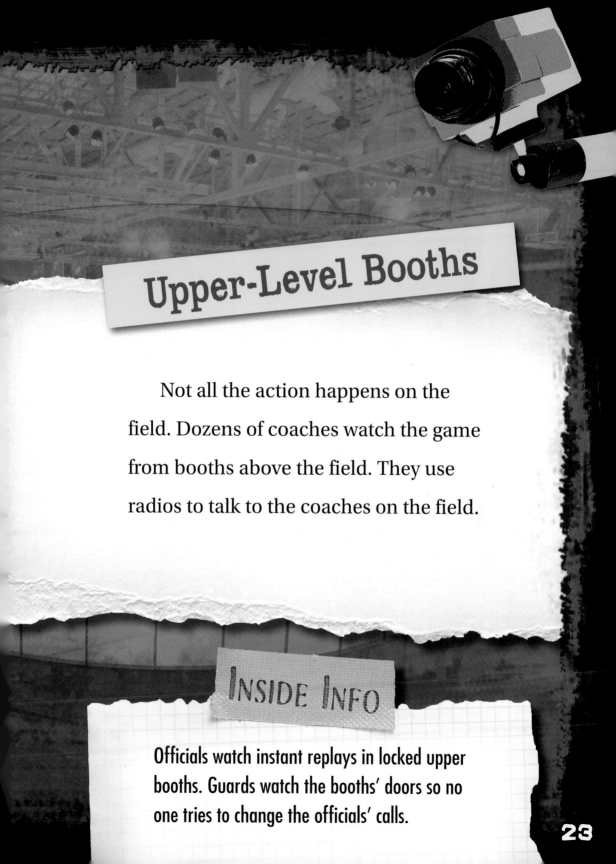

Upper-Level Booths

Not all the action happens on the field. Dozens of coaches watch the game from booths above the field. They use radios to talk to the coaches on the field.

INSIDE INFO

Officials watch instant replays in locked upper booths. Guards watch the booths' doors so no one tries to change the officials' calls.

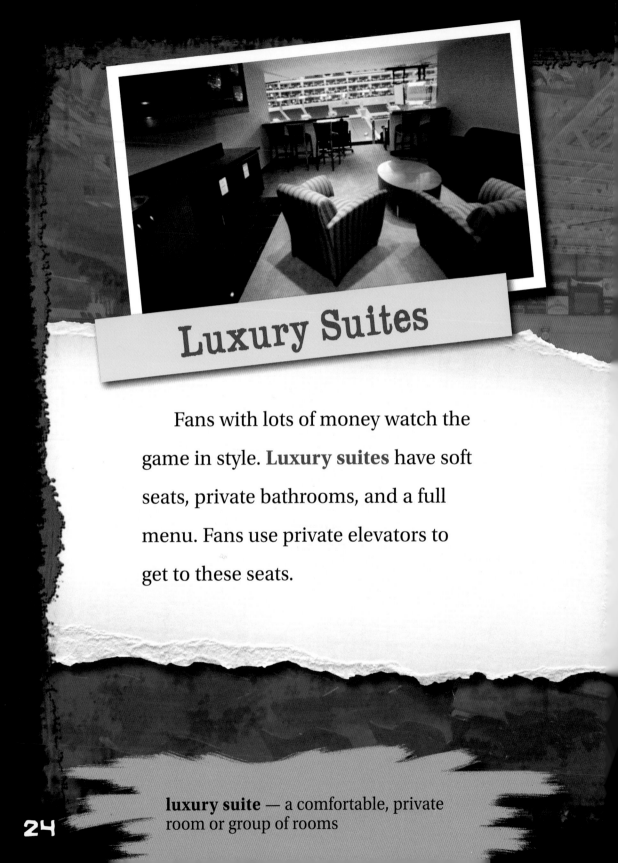

Luxury Suites

Fans with lots of money watch the game in style. **Luxury suites** have soft seats, private bathrooms, and a full menu. Fans use private elevators to get to these seats.

luxury suite — a comfortable, private room or group of rooms

INSIDE INFO

People pay more than $1 million to watch games from a luxury suite.

STADIUM SECRETS

A lot of action happens on the field at a sports stadium. But even more action happens off the field.

Next time you go to a sports stadium, look down the long halls. Behind the scoreboards and lights lies the hidden world that keeps the stadium running.

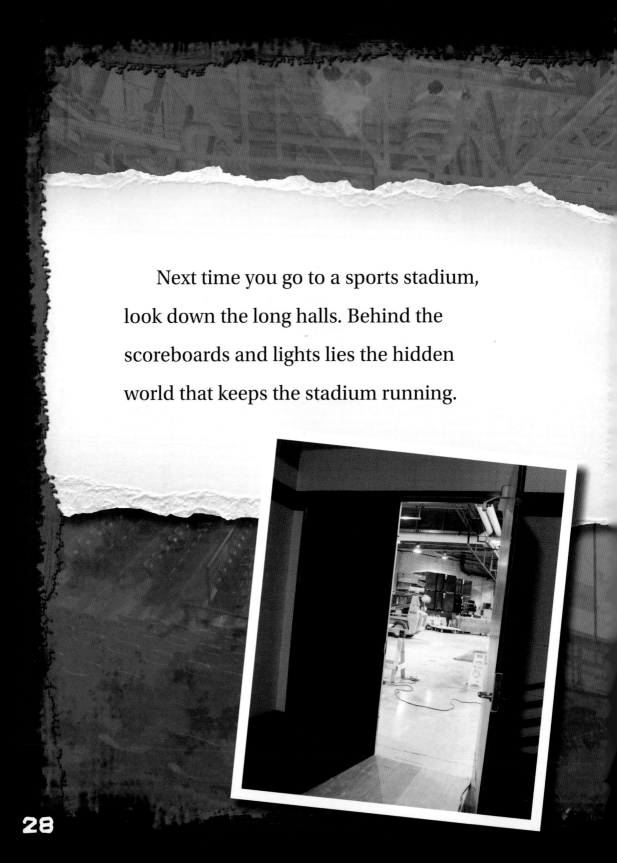

GLOSSARY

broadcast center (BRAWD-kast SEN-tur) — the place in the stadium that sends out programs to TV or radio stations

concession stand (kuhn-SESH-uhn STAND) — an area where food and drinks can be purchased

luxury suite (LUHK-shuh-ree SWEET) — a comfortable, private room or group of rooms

maintenance (MAYN-tuh-nuhnss) — the upkeep of machines or a building

monitor (MON-uh-tur) — a TV or computer screen that is used to show what is being recorded

security (si-KYER-i-tee) — safety; security is also a department whose task it is to provide protection.

READ MORE

Curlee, Lynn. *Ballpark: The Story of America's Baseball Fields.* New York: Atheneum Books for Young Readers, 2005.

Encarnacion, Elizabeth. *Sports Stadiums.* QEB Buildings at Work. Lagune Hills, Calif.: QEB, 2007.

Owens, Thomas S. *Football Stadiums.* Sports Palaces. Brookfield, Conn.: Millbrook Press, 2001.

INTERNET SITES

FactHound offers a safe, fun way to find Internet sites related to this book. All of the sites on FactHound have been researched by our staff.

Here's all you do:

Visit *www.facthound.com*

FactHound will fetch the best sites for you!

INDEX